SCHOLASTIC

DECIMALS & PERCENTS

PRACTICE PUZZLES

40 Reproducible Solve-the-Riddle Activity Pages
That Help All Kids Master Decimals and Percents

by Bob Hugel

NEW YORK • TORONTO • LONDON • AUCKLAND • SYDNEY
MEXICO CITY • NEW DELHI • HONG KONG • BUENOS AIRES

Teaching *Resources*

Dedication

To Mike and Debbie, a great brother-and-sister team

Cover design by Maria Lilja
Cover illustration by Kelly Kennedy
Interior design by Holly Grundon
Interior illustrations by Kelly Kennedy

ISBN 0-439-71857-0
Copyright © 2005 by Bob Hugel
All rights reserved.
Printed in the U.S.A.

1 2 3 4 5 6 7 8 9 10   40   12 11 10 09 08 07 06 05

Contents

Introduction

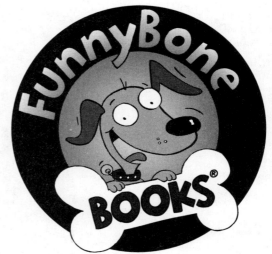

Welcome to *FunnyBone Books: Decimals & Percents Practice Puzzles*, a surefire way to get students excited about math. This book combines decimal and percent problems with loads of hilarious riddles guaranteed to get students revved up for learning.

As you may know, one of the keys to helping students learn successfully is to make learning fun. That's why each page of *Decimals & Percents Practice Puzzles* starts with an amusing riddle. We hope your students will be motivated to solve the math problems because the answers will help them find the rib-tickling solution to each riddle.

Along the way, your students will get drilled on several decimal skills, including rounding, comparing, adding and subtracting decimals that are in different places, and multiplying and dividing decimals. They'll also get practice solving money math problems and working with percents. Finally, they'll convert fractions to decimals, decimals to fractions, and decimals to percents.

We hope your students enjoy *Decimals & Percents Practice Puzzles* and benefit from the skills presented in this book. By making math enjoyable, we hope to reveal a terrific secret to your students—math is lots of fun!

NAME _____ DATE _____

Riddle 1

What do you call a tree root with four equal sides?

What To Do

Answer the questions below. Match each answer to a letter in the Key. Then write the letter in the space above its problem number to find the answer to the riddle.

1 Circle the numeral in the **ones** place: **5.8**

2 Circle the numeral in the **tenths** place: **5.08**

3 Circle the numeral in the **hundredths** place: **4.26**

4 Circle the numeral in the **tenths** place: **32.75**

5 Circle the numeral in the **hundredths** place: **461.925**

6 Circle the numeral in the **tens** place: **83.403**

7 Circle the numeral in the **hundreds** place: **495.893**

8 Circle the numeral in the **thousandths** place: **2.691**

9 Circle the numeral in the **hundredths** place: **753.4362**

10 Circle the numeral in the **thousandths** place: **4.12967**

Key

8	E		3	R
0	O		1	Q
6	A		4	U
5	S		7	R
9	T		2	O

Riddle Answer

A __ __ __ __ __ __   __ __ __ __

NAME_____ DATE_____

Riddle 2

Why did the farmer want the tree, instead of his dog, to guard his sheep?

What To Do

Round each decimal to the nearest whole number.
Match each answer to a letter in the Key. Then write the letter in the
space above its problem number to find the answer to the riddle.

1 1.7 = _____   **6** 9.8 = _____

2 5.3 = _____   **7** 12.4 = _____

3 8.4 = _____   **8** 9.1 = _____

4 3.6 = _____   **9** 20.3 = _____

5 1.3 = _____   **10** 14.2 = _____

Key

3 . . . . U	14 . . . . D	10 . . . . O
9 . . . . R	7 . . . . N	20 . . . . B
6 C	1 . . . . A	2 . . . . K
4 . . . . A	5 . . . . E	12 . . . . M
8 . . . . R	13 . . . . J	21 I

Riddle Answer

The tree h __ __   __ __ __ __   __ __ __ __.
       4 **10**   **7** **6** **8** **2**   **9** **5** **3** **1**

NAME_____ DATE_____

Riddle 3

What did the blanket say to the bed?

What To Do

Round each decimal to the nearest 10th place.
Match each answer to a letter in the Key. Then write the letter in the
space above its problem number to find the answer to the riddle.

1   2.39 = _____

2   6.76 = _____

3   5.12 = _____

4   10.84 = _____

5   1.91 = _____

6   17.23 = _____

7   25.48 = _____

8   8.26 = _____

9   30.07 = _____

10   12.66 = _____

Key

8.3	D	30	M	5.2	B
1.9	C	12.7	O	10.9	F
12.6	A	5.1	R	6.8	Y
2.4	U	10.8	E	17.2	O
25.5	E	30.1	V	8.2	W

Riddle Answer

"I've got ___ ___ ___   ___ ___ ___ ___ ___ ___ ___."

2 **6** **1**   **5** **10** **9** **7** **3** **4** **8**

NAME_____ DATE _____

Riddle 4

Why did the Earth make the sun dizzy?

What To Do

Round each decimal to the nearest 100th place.
Match each answer to a letter in the Key. Then write the letter in the
space above its problem number to find the answer to the riddle.

1 5.257 = _____   **6** 2.163 = _____

2 7.846 = _____   **7** 15.782 = _____

3 10.629 = _____   **8** 1.367 = _____

4 8.474 = _____   **9** 20.554 = _____

5 3.991 = _____   **10** 9.123 = _____

Key

1.37 L	2.16 I	5.25 . . . . O
10.62 . . . . F	5.26 I	10.63 . . . . E
2.17 . . . . A	15.80 . . . . K	8.48 . . . . B
7.85 C	9.12 C	3.99 . . . . D
15.78 . . . . S	8.47 . . . . N	20.55 . . . . R

Riddle Answer

It went aroun ___ ___ ___ ___ ___ ___ ___ ___ ___ ___.

5 **1** **4** **10** **6** **9** **2** **8** **3** **7**

NAME _____ DATE _____

Riddle 5

What did the bee say before eating its favorite meal?

What To Do

In each problem, circle the decimal that is greater. Match each answer to a letter in the Key. Then write the letter in the space above its problem number to find the answer to the riddle.

1 6.2 or 5.7

2 3.1 or 2.9

3 4.45 or 4.48

4 7.6 or 7.63

5 9.071 or 9.08

6 15.4 or 14.5

7 5.658 or 5.649

8 20.83 or 20.099

9 32.364 or 32.461

10 75.014 or 75.1

Key

7.63 . . . . N	20.099 V	15.4 . . . . K
9.08 . . . . Y	9.071 . . . . . . R	5.658 . . . . . . N
6.2 . . . . E	3.1 . . . . H	75.014 . . . . . . T
75.1 . . . . H	32.461 . . . . . . S	5.649 . . . . . . G
4.48 . . . . A	2.9 X	20.83 . . . . . . O

Riddle Answer

"T __ __ __ __ __ , __ __ __ __ __ !"
10 **3** **4** **6** **9**   **2** **8** **7** **1** **5**

NAME _____ DATE _____

Riddle 6

How can the pots tell when the kettle is mad?

What To Do

Convert the fractions below into decimals. Match each answer to a letter in the Key. Then write the letter in the space above its problem number to find the answer to the riddle.

1 $\frac{1}{10}$ = _____

2 $\frac{5}{10}$ = _____

3 $\frac{7}{10}$ = _____

4 $\frac{18}{100}$ = _____

5 $\frac{25}{100}$ = _____

6 $\frac{1}{100}$ = _____

7 $\frac{60}{100}$ = _____

8 $\frac{99}{100}$ = _____

9 $\frac{463}{1,000}$ = _____

10 $\frac{3}{1,000}$ = _____

Key

0.5 . . . . S	0.05 V	0.25 . . . . M
0.18 . . . . S	4.63 . . . . N	0.06 L
0.01 . . . . T	0.463 . . . . W	0.03 I
0.99 . . . . . E	0.3 . . . . G	0.6 . . . . O
0.003 . . . . . . A	0.1 . . . . B	0.7 L

Riddle Answer

It ___ ___ ___ ___ ___ off ___ ___ ___ ___ ___.
  1 **3** **7** **9** **2**   **4** **6** **8** **10** **5**

NAME_____ DATE_____

Riddle 7

What did the rabbit say to get the other rabbits moving?

What To Do

Convert the fractions below into decimals. Match each answer to a letter in the Key. Then write the letter in the space above its problem number to find the answer to the riddle.

1 $\frac{2}{5}$ = _____

2 $\frac{3}{12}$ = _____

3 $\frac{19}{38}$ = _____

4 $\frac{1}{8}$ = _____

5 $\frac{7}{10}$ = _____

6 $\frac{5}{25}$ = _____

7 $\frac{6}{100}$ = _____

8 $\frac{42}{80}$ = _____

9 $\frac{27}{36}$ = _____

10 $\frac{6}{200}$ = _____

Key

0.125 . . . . . . T	0.525 . . . . . . T	0.03 . . . . P
0.2 . . . . E	0.25 . . . . O	0.04 . . . . B
0.7 . . . . T	0.6 . . . . A	0.75 . . . . . . H
0.4 L	0.3 . . . . W	0.06 I
0.8 . . . . G	0.575 . . . Z	0.5 . . . . O

Riddle Answer

" ___ ___ ___ 's ___ ___ ___ ___ ___ ___ ___ !"

NAME _____ DATE _____

Riddle 8

What did the cow say to the tractor that was blocking its path?

What To Do

Convert the decimals below into fractions. Write your answers in simplest terms. Match each answer to a letter in the Key. Then write the letter in the space above its problem number to find the answer to the riddle.

1 0.1 = _____   **6** 0.6 = _____

2 0.3 = _____   **7** 0.25 = _____

3 0.5 = _____   **8** 0.37 = _____

4 0.8 = _____   **9** 0.46 = _____

5 0.2 = _____   **10** 0.12 = _____

Key

$1/25$ . . . . . . W	$1/4$ . . . . O	$4/5$ . . . . E
$1/100$ . . . . . R	$3/25$ . . . . . . E	$1/10$ . . . . . . M
$3/10$ . . . . . . S	$23/50$ L	$5/100$ . . . . . N
$1/12$ I	$46/1,000$ . . . U	$3/5$ . . . . O
$1/5$ . . . . A	$1/2$ . . . . E	$37/100$ V

Riddle Answer

"P __ __ __ __ __ __ __ __ __ – __ __."
  9 4 5 2 10   1 6 7   8 3

NAME_____ DATE _____

Riddle 9

Why did the window succeed in business?

What To Do

Convert the mixed numbers below into decimals. Match each answer to a letter in the Key. Then write the letter in the space above its problem number to find the answer to the riddle.

1 $5\frac{1}{10}$ = _____

2 $4\frac{7}{10}$ = _____

3 $26\frac{5}{10}$ = _____

4 $12\frac{45}{100}$ = _____

5 $35\frac{16}{100}$ = _____

6 $67\frac{8}{100}$ = _____

7 $95\frac{48}{100}$ = _____

8 $17\frac{31}{1,000}$ = _____

9 $59\frac{675}{1,000}$ = _____

10 $186\frac{5}{1,000}$ = _____

Key

35.16 . . . . E		5.1 . . . . S		12.45 . . . . A	
26.5 . . . . W		17.031 . . . . P		186.005 L	
59.675 . . . . Y		17.31 I		95.48 . . . . A	
186.5 C		67.08 . . . . O		5.01 . . . . D	
12.045 . . . . . . F		4.7 . . . . N		67.800 . . . . . . B	

Riddle Answer

It was ___ ___ ___ ___ ___ ___   ___ ___ ___ ___.

④ ⑩ ③ ⑦ ⑨ ① ⑥ ⑧ ⑤ ②

NAME_____ DATE _____

Riddle 10

What is a dog's favorite type of clothing?

What To Do

Convert the mixed numbers below into decimals. Match each answer to a letter in the Key. Then write the letter in the space above its problem number to find the answer to the riddle.

1 $4\frac{1}{2}$ = _____

2 $1\frac{3}{4}$ = _____

3 $5\frac{4}{5}$ = _____

4 $2\frac{3}{10}$ = _____

5 $10\frac{1}{4}$ = _____

6 $8\frac{7}{8}$ = _____

7 $12\frac{5}{8}$ = _____

8 $3\frac{15}{20}$ = _____

9 $6\frac{20}{40}$ = _____

10 $20\frac{8}{20}$ = _____

Key

8.875 . . . . . . A	3.2 . . . . D	5.8 . . . . A
10.5 . . . . B	1.75 . . . . A	3.75 I
12.625 . . . . . T	10.25 . . . . . . N	6.5 . . . . S
2.3 . . . . P	5.4 . . . . M	6.25 . . . . E
20.4 . . . . R	4.5 . . . . P	12.725 . . . . . W

Riddle Answer

 of

NAME_____   DATE _____

Riddle 11

Why was the tired criminal glad when the cops came?

What To Do

In each problem, circle the fraction or decimal that is greater. Match each answer to a letter in the Key. Then write the letter in the space above its problem number to find the answer to the riddle.

1 $\frac{8}{16}$ or **0.58**   **6** $\frac{14}{56}$ or **0.22**

2 $\frac{3}{4}$ or **0.72**   **7** $\frac{7}{8}$ or **0.785**

3 $\frac{6}{10}$ or **0.49**   **8** $\frac{15}{40}$ or **0.357**

4 $\frac{9}{20}$ or **0.16**   **9** $\frac{1}{10}$ or **0.001**

5 $\frac{24}{30}$ or **0.93**   **10** $\frac{26}{50}$ or **0.536**

Key

0.93 . . . . S	8/16 V	3/4 . . . . D
24/30 . . . . . . M	0.536 . . . . . . E	0.785 . . . . K
7/8 . . . . R	0.001 . . . . . . Q	1/10 . . . . T
0.58 . . . . E	0.49 . . . . B	15/40 . . . . . . R
9/20 . . . . A	14/56 . . . . . . N	6/10 . . . . R

Riddle Answer

He was now u __ __ __ __   __ __   __ __ __ __.
⑥ ② ⑩ ⑧   ④ ③   ⑦ ① ⑤ ⑨

NAME _____   DATE _____

Riddle 12

Why did the phone stop calling the answering machine?

What To Do

Solve the addition problems below. Match each answer
to a letter in the Key. Then write the letter in the space above its problem
number to find the answer to the riddle.

1 1 + 0.5 = _____

2 4 + 0.6 = _____

3 8 + 0.9 + 0.01 = _____

4 5 + 0.8 + 0.03 = _____

5 0.2 + 0.09 = _____

6 0.4 + 0.07 = _____

7 7 + 0.1 + 0.02 + 0.004 = _____

8 9 + 0.6 + 0.05 + 0.008 = _____

9 80 + 3 + 0.06 + 0.005 = _____

10 10 + 0.003 = _____

Key

8.91 . . . . E	83.65 . . . . B	5.83 . . . . D
10.3 . . . . T	7.124 . . . . S	1.5 . . . . E
0.029 I	0.29 . . . . E	4.6 . . . . G
9.658 . . . . . . M	10.003 . . . . A	0.47 . . . . S
4.07 . . . . N	83.065 . . . . S	1.05 . . . . O

Riddle Answer

It never return __ __   __ __ __ __ __ __ __ __ __ .

NAME_____ DATE _____

Riddle 13

Why was the bird afraid to fly?

What To Do

Solve the addition problems below. Match each answer
to a letter in the Key. Then write the letter in the space above its problem
number to find the answer to the riddle.

1 3 + 1.4 = _____

2 6 + 2.7 = _____

3 8 + 5.5 = _____

4 4 + 9.3 = _____

5 5 + 6.1 = _____

6 10 + 8.25 = _____

7 2 + 14.67 = _____

8 20 + 3.93 = _____

9 11 + 17.542 = _____

10 25 + 16.816 = _____

Key

13.5 . . . . S	4.4 . . . . W	6.6 . . . . K
16.67 . . . . A	418.16 I	18.25 . . . . R
11.1 . . . . D	28.542 C	13.3 C
23.93 . . . . . . E	9.3 . . . . M	8.7 . . . . R
9.7 L	41.816 . . . . . . O	14.3 . . . . P

Riddle Answer

It was a __ __ __ __ __ __ __ - __ __ __ __.

NAME_____ DATE_____

Riddle 14

Why did the salad feel naked?

What To Do

Solve the addition problems below. Match each answer to a letter in the Key. Then write the letter in the space above its problem number to find the answer to the riddle.

1 0.4 + 0.3 = _____

2 0.8 + 0.2 = _____

3 0.5 + 0.6 = _____

4 0.2 + 0.6 = _____

5 0.3 + 0.9 = _____

6 10.1 + 8.7 = _____

7 15.6 + 1.8 = _____

8 9.9 + 3.5 = _____

9 20.7 + 15.4 = _____

10 8.4 + 33.9 = _____

Key

18.8 . . . . D	0.11 . . . . H	0.12 . . . . . . W
0.7 . . . . R	41.13 . . . . O	16.14 . . . . K
1.2 . . . . E	1 . . . . N	1.1 . . . . S
35.1 . . . . Q	0.8 . . . . G	42.3 . . . . Y
36.1 . . . . S	17.4 I	13.4 . . . . N

Riddle Answer

It didn't have a __ __ __ __ __ __ __ __ __ __ __ .

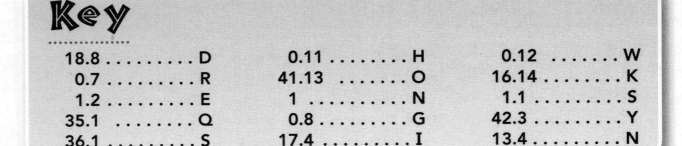

NAME_____ DATE_____

Riddle 15

Which planet won the singing contest?

What To Do

Solve the addition problems below. Match each answer to a letter in the Key. Then write the letter in the space above its problem number to find the answer to the riddle.

1 0.46 + 0.21 = _____

2 0.35 + 0.35 = _____

3 6.48 + 3.42 = _____

4 10.72 + 2.15 = _____

5 9.59 + 8.67 = _____

6 0.174 + 0.503 = _____

7 0.892 + 0.982 = _____

8 16.066 + 1.338 = _____

9 5.249 + 22.916 = _____

10 18.451 + 13.547 = _____

Key

0.67 . . . . S	0.1874 . . . . . . D	16.39 I
17.26 . . . . K	31.998 . . . . P	12.78 . . . . O
9.9 . . . . N	0.7 . . . . U	27.15 X
1.874 . . . . . . E	0.677 . . . . . . E	28.165 . . . . . . W
18.26 . . . . A	12.87 . . . . N	17.404 . . . . . . T

Riddle Answer

It ___ ___ ___ ___ ___ ___ - ___ ___ ___ ___.
    9 **5** **1** **4** **6** **10** **8** **2** **3** **7**

NAME_____ DATE_____

Riddle 16

Why was the hockey player always in trouble?

What To Do

Solve the addition problems below. Match each answer to a letter in the Key. Then write the letter in the space above its problem number to find the answer to the riddle.

1 0.23 + 3.4 = _____

2 0.456 + 0.25 = _____

3 7.2 + 8.68 = _____

4 0.129 + 0.47 = _____

5 1.53 + 0.397 = _____

6 27.4 + 0.352 + 5.06 = _____

7 0.486 + 13.9 + 0.71 = _____

8 100.8 + 8.75 + 0.324 = _____

9 73.1 + 0.112 + 20.53 = _____

10 3.368 + 26.28 + 23.7 = _____

Key

15.096 . . . . T	5.7 . . . . G	3.63 . . . . O
109.874 . . . . E	0.481 L	32.812 I
93.742 . . . . H	0.599 . . . . N	6.96 . . . . B
0.706 . . . . N	15.88 . . . . D	289.6 . . . . U
53.348 I	9.4 . . . . A	1.927 C

Riddle Answer

He skate ___ ___ ___ ___ ___ ___ ___ ___ ___ ___ ___ ___.

NAME_____ DATE _____

Riddle 17

Why is it hard to listen to a circle speak?

What To Do

In each problem below, estimate the sums to a reasonable whole number. Match each answer to a letter in the Key. Then write the letter in the space above its problem number to find the answer to the riddle.

1 6.6 + 7.1 = _____

2 1.4 + 2.8 = _____

3 5.3 + 1.9 = _____

4 3.1 + 11.8 = _____

5 8.3 + 9.9 = _____

6 0.11 + 2.68 = _____

7 5.24 + 3.67 = _____

8 7.55 + 3.47 = _____

9 35.18 + 8.67 = _____

10 104.62 + 104.47 = _____

Key

3 . . . . H	209 . . . . N	6 I
44 . . . . T	11 . . . . O	13 . . . . P
15 . . . . T	4 . . . . O	2 . . . . M
14 I	18 . . . . E	43 . . . . D
7 . . . . P	9 . . . . T	208 . . . . H

Riddle Answer

It never gets __ __ __ __ __ __ __ __ __ __ .

4 **8** **7** **6** **5** **3** **2** **1** **10** **9**

NAME _____ DATE _____

Riddle 18

What did the shovel say to the sick bucket?

What To Do

Solve the subtraction problems below. Match each answer to a letter in the Key. Then write the letter in the space above its problem number to find the answer to the riddle.

1 0.4 – 0.3 = _____

2 0.5 – 0.1 = _____

3 0.7 – 0.5 = _____

4 0.8 – 0.3 = _____

5 0.9 – 0.2 = _____

6 10.6 – 7.6 = _____

7 12.9 – 8.2 = _____

8 4.4 – 3.6 = _____

9 3.7 – 1.9 = _____

10 15.4 – 9.8 = _____

Key

0.2 . . . . O	1 . . . . A	5.6 L
0.8 . . . . K	0.5 . . . . A	3 . . . . U
4.7 . . . . P	3.6 . . . . W	0.4 . . . . O
0.7 . . . . O	0.1 I	1.2 . . . . O
6.4 . . . . R	1.8 L	6.6 . . . . Z

Riddle Answer

"Y __ __ __ __ __ __ __ __ __ __ __ __!"
3 6   9 2 5 8   7 4 1 10

NAME_____ DATE _____

Riddle 19

Why did the horse keep stopping?

What To Do

Solve the subtraction problems below. Match each answer to a letter in the Key. Then write the letter in the space above its problem number to find the answer to the riddle.

1 5.5 – 4 = _____

2 8.3 – 6 = _____

3 2.7 – 1 = _____

4 6.4 – 2 = _____

5 10.6 – 3 = _____

6 12.9 – 10 = _____

7 9.3 – 5 = _____

8 20.1 – 11 = _____

9 8.8 – 8 = _____

10 25.2 – 14 = _____

Key

3.4 . . . . R	4.3 . . . . O	2.6 . . . . F
1.8 . . . . P	11.2 . . . . T	6.7 . . . . E
7.6 I	5.5 . . . . W	1.7 I
1.5 . . . . S	2.3 . . . . N	4.4 . . . . A
0.8 L	9.1 L	2.9 . . . . T

Riddle Answer

___ ___ **was a** ___ ___ ___ ___ ___ – ___ ___ ___ .

NAME _____ DATE _____

Riddle 20

Why was the shirt sad?

What To Do

Solve the subtraction problems below. Match each answer to a letter in the Key.
Then write the letter in the space above its problem number to find
the answer to the riddle.

1 6 – 1.5 = _____

2 8 – 4.2 = _____

3 5 – 3.3 = _____

4 10 – 6.4 = _____

5 16 – 13.1 = _____

6 20 – 7.8 = _____

7 33 – 10.6 = _____

8 50 – 2.7 = _____

9 45 – 40.9 = _____

10 76 – 29.3 = _____

Key

4.5 .... S	46.7 L	13.2 .... D
5.5 .... R	4.2 .... O	7.5 .... K
12.2 .... E	3.8 .... U	24.2 .... Q
1.7 .... B	2.9 I	47.3 .... E
3.6 .... A	22.4 .... T	4.1 .... W

Riddle Answer

Becaus ___ ___ ___ ___ ___ ___ ___ ___ ___ ___ .

8 **5 7** **9 4 1** **3 10 2 6**

NAME_____ DATE_____

Riddle 21

What do boxers do before going to bed?

What To Do

Solve the subtraction problems below. Match each answer to a letter in the Key.
Then write the letter in the space above its problem number to find
the answer to the riddle.

1 0.44 – 0.22 = _____   **6** 9.43 – 6.19 = _____

2 0.26 – 0.16 = _____   **7** 20.11 – 5.03 = _____

3 0.89 – 0.37 = _____   **8** 6.25 – 3.86 = _____

4 0.957 – 0.925 = _____   **9** 30.625 – 20.263 = _____

5 1.538 – 0.724 = _____   **10** 8.917 – 8.572 = _____

Key

2.39	F	15.08	H	0.052	P
0.032	I	0.52	L	8.14	A
3.24	O	0.32	E	0.1	T
0.345	G	15.8	G	0.814	L
0.239	V	0.22	I	10.362	W

Riddle Answer

They have a p ___ ___ ___ ___ ___ ___ ___ ___ ___ ___ .

NAME_____ DATE _____

Riddle 22

Why did the father keep giving his children candy?

What To Do

Solve the subtraction problems below. Match each answer to a letter in the Key. Then write the letter in the space above its problem number to find the answer to the riddle.

1 11.54 – 5.1 = _____   **6** 65.75 – 31.812 = _____

2 20.1 – 5.04 = _____   **7** 50.376 – 41.6 = _____

3 5.6 – 1.29 = _____   **8** 27.2 – 9.99 = _____

4 16.92 – 7.5 = _____   **9** 30.1 – 18.831 = _____

5 8.864 – 3.41 = _____   **10** 10.8 – 6.522 = _____

Key

8.776 I	15.06 . . . . S	4.31 . . . . O
5.454 . . . . A	33.938 . . . . P	4.278 . . . . O
15.14 . . . . K	42.78 . . . . U	17.19 . . . . E
6.44 . . . . P	33.942 . . . . W	11.269 L
17.21 L	9.42 L	4.49 . . . . N

Riddle Answer

He wa ___ ___ ___ ___ ___ ___ ___ - ___ ___ ___.
    2   **5**   **8** **10** **4** **9** **7**   **1** **3** **6**

NAME _____ DATE _____

Riddle 23

Why didn't anyone trust the lamp?

What To Do

Solve the multiplication problems below. Match each answer to a letter in the Key. Then write the letter in the space above its problem number to find the answer to the riddle.

1 1 x 0.2 = _____

2 10 x 0.4 = _____

3 6 x 0.7 = _____

4 10 x 4.8 = _____

5 7 x 10.3 = _____

6 2 x 9.5 = _____

7 3 x 12.6 = _____

8 1 x 18.9 = _____

9 2 x 25.5 = _____

10 9 x 8.2 = _____

Key

10 . . . . M	19 . . . . Y	71.2 . . . . O
38.7 . . . . W	53 I	19.8 . . . . U
37.8 . . . . A	0.2 . . . . S	4.2 . . . . T
72.1 . . . . D	48 . . . . H	18.9 . . . . A
4 . . . . W	51 I	73.8 . . . . S

Riddle Answer

___ ___ ___ ___ ___ ___ ___ ___ ___ ___ ___ .
9 **3**   **2** **8** **10**   **1** **4** **7** **5** **6**

NAME_____ DATE _____

Riddle 24

What fruit is round, red, and always puts its best foot forward?

What To Do

Solve the multiplication problems below. Match each answer to a letter in the Key. Then write the letter in the space above its problem number to find the answer to the riddle.

1 6.43 x 5 = _____   **6** 1.62 x 35 = _____

2 2.95 x 4 = _____   **7** 7.18 x 16 = _____

3 5.08 x 6 = _____   **8** 10.46 x 22 = _____

4 9.36 x 10 = _____   **9** 5.25 x 40 = _____

5 4.88 x 20 = _____   **10** 3.57 x 100 = _____

Key

114.88 . . . . T	93.6 . . . . T	11.8 . . . . E
97.6 . . . . O	357 . . . . D	35.7 I
32.15 . . . . E	230.12 . . . . O	56.7 . . . . R
1.18 . . . . N	30.48 . . . . M	210 . . . . A
21 . . . . U	9.36 X	3.215 . . . . . . B

Riddle Answer

A __ __ __   __ __ __ __ - __ __ __
 6 **1** **10** **4** **8** **3** **9** **7** **5** **2**

NAME_____ DATE _____

Riddle 25

What did the dog say to the other dog before sharing his food?

What To Do

Solve the multiplication problems below. Match each answer to a letter in the Key. Then write the letter in the space above its problem number to find the answer to the riddle.

1 0.5 x 0.5 = _____

2 0.8 x 0.4 = _____

3 0.2 x 0.7 = _____

4 0.3 x 1.9 = _____

5 0.6 x 3.3 = _____

6 4.9 x 0.8 = _____

7 2.1 x 2.5 = _____

8 3.61 x 4.78 = _____

9 12.57 x 3.28 = _____

10 17.82 x 2.43 = _____

Key

3.92 . . . . . . P	0.32 I	1,725.58 X
41.2296 . . . . . A	52.5 . . . . K	17.2558 . . . . . O
1.98 . . . . . . P	3.2 . . . . U	5.25 . . . . T
43.3026 . . . . . E	0.14 . . . . . . T	0.25 . . . . . . N
2.5 . . . . . . W	39.2 L	0.57 . . . . E

Riddle Answer

"B ___ ___ ___ ___ ___ ___ ___ ___ ___ ___ ___ !"

8 **1** **10**   **9** **5** **6** **4** **7** **2** **3**

NAME _____ **DATE** _____

Riddle 26

Why did the truck quit working at the construction site?

What To Do

Solve the multiplication problems below. Match each answer to a letter in the Key. Then write the letter in the space above its problem number to find the answer to the riddle.

1 0.5 x 0.73 = _____

2 0.4 x 0.16 = _____

3 0.7 x 0.243 = _____

4 2.3 x 0.388 = _____

5 7.6 x 1.451 = _____

6 0.167 x 7.3 = _____

7 2.082 x 2.5 = _____

8 3.333 x 11.15 = _____

9 8.096 x 3.71 = _____

10 1.48 x 6.464 = _____

Key

11.0276 . . . . . . N	1.2191 . . . . . . P	12.191 . . . . . . K
9.56672 . . . . . D	0.365 . . . . U	30.03616 . . . . . D
37.16295 . . . . . E	6.4 C	5.205 . . . . N
3.65 I	110.276 . . . . . . F	1.701 . . . . . . A
0.064 . . . . . . O	0.8924 . . . . . . G	0.1701 . . . . . M

Riddle Answer

It was tired of bei __ __ __ __ __ __ __ __ __ __ __ __ __ .

   1 **3** **6** **8** **10** **2** **7**

NAME _____ DATE _____

Riddle 27

Why was the fish asked to tell jokes?

What To Do

Solve the division problems below. Match each answer to a letter in the Key. Then write the letter in the space above its problem number to find the answer to the riddle.

1 5 ÷ 0.5 = _____

2 12 ÷ 1.5 = _____

3 33 ÷ 2.2 = _____

4 66 ÷ 3.3 = _____

5 105 ÷ 4.2 = _____

6 120 ÷ 7.5 = _____

7 265 ÷ 5.3 = _____

8 114 ÷ 9.5 = _____

9 546 ÷ 8.4 = _____

10 372 ÷ 12.4 = _____

Key

20 . . . . H	75 . . . . D	42 . . . . Z
8 I	5 . . . . B	16 L
12 . . . . A	15 . . . . W	65 . . . . F
100 . . . . P	50 . . . . N	80 . . . . M
25 . . . . O	30 C	10 . . . . S

Riddle Answer

It was ___ ___ ___ ___ ___ ___ ___ ___ ___ ___ ___.
    8   **10** **6** **5** **3** **7** **9** **2** **1** **4**

NAME_____ DATE_____

Riddle 28

What did the elephant say about the flies?

What To Do

Solve the division problems below. Match each answer to a letter in the Key. Then write the letter in the space above its problem number to find the answer to the riddle.

1 0.1 ÷ 0.5 = _____   **6** 20.1 ÷ 0.3 = _____

2 0.5 ÷ 0.2 = _____   **7** 12.5 ÷ 2.5 = _____

3 3.8 ÷ 0.8 = _____   **8** 30.4 ÷ 3.2 = _____

4 2.4 ÷ 0.6 = _____   **9** 50.15 ÷ 14.75 = _____

5 14.7 ÷ 2.4 = _____   **10** 66.56 ÷ 10.24 = _____

Key

2.5 L		0.2 . . . . M		5 . . . . Y	
6.125 . . . . G		1 . . . . N		6.7 . . . . R	
9.5 . . . . B		3.4 . . . . A		6.5 L	
2 . . . . O		67 . . . . E		4.75 . . . . E	
4 . . . . U		0.475 . . . . P		0.4 I	

Riddle Answer

"They r ___ ___ ___ ___ ___ ___ ___ ___ ___ ___ ___ ___!"
    6 **9** **10** **2** **7**   **8** **4** **5**   **1** **3**

NAME_____ DATE_____

Riddle 29

Why do frogs celebrate every four years?

What To Do

Solve the division problems below. Match each answer to a letter in the Key. Then write the letter in the space above its problem number to find the answer to the riddle.

1 12.4 ÷ 3.2 = _____

2 20.8 ÷ 5.2 = _____

3 28.75 ÷ 4.6 = _____

4 18.24 ÷ 1.5 = _____

5 67.248 ÷ 7.2 = _____

6 93.651 ÷ 9.3 = _____

7 17.6112 ÷ 2.4 = _____

8 165.645 ÷ 0.81 = _____

9 35.8918 ÷ 0.62 = _____

10 141.328 ÷ 0.44 = _____

Key

20.45 . . . . N	321.2 . . . . R	6.25 . . . . E
10.07 . . . . . . E	6.52 . . . . . . O	9.34 . . . . . . T
12.16 . . . . . . P	3.875 . . . . . . A	57.89 . . . . Y
9.43 . . . . . M	12.61 . . . . U	5.789 . . . . . K
7.338 L	4 I	204.5 . . . . A

Riddle Answer

 's

NAME _____ DATE _____

Riddle 30

Why did the tree that was in business grow more limbs?

What To Do

Convert the decimals below to percents. Match each answer to a letter in the Key. Then write the letter in the space above its problem number to find the answer to the riddle.

1 0.3 = _____   **6** 0.06 = _____

2 0.15 = _____   **7** 0.97 = _____

3 0.07 = _____   **8** 0.375 = _____

4 0.29 = _____   **9** 0.861 = _____

5 0.41 = _____   **10** 0.012 = _____

Key

86.1% . . . . N	37.5% . . . . O	70% . . . . M
7% . . . . . . R	3% . . . . D	375% . . . . Y
6% C	60% . . . . W	15% . . . . . . H
12% I	1.2% . . . . . . B	41% . . . . U
30% . . . . A	97% . . . . T	29% . . . . O

Riddle Answer

It wanted t ___ ___ ___ ___ ___ ___ ___ ___ ___ ___.

⑧   ⑩ ③ ① ⑨ ⑥ ②   ④ ⑤ ⑦

NAME_____ DATE _____

Riddle 31

Which vegetable listens well?

What To Do

Convert the percents below into decimals. Match each answer to a letter in the Key. Then write the letter in the space above its problem number to find the answer to the riddle.

1 52% = _____   **6** 11.5% = _____

2 88% = _____   **7** 26.2% = _____

3 73% = _____   **8** 38.7% = _____

4 4% = _____   **9** 99.9% = _____

5 9% = _____   **10** 43.19% = _____

Key

0.73 . . . . F	0.88 . . . . O	0.4319 . . . . . A
0.262 . . . . . . E	0.04 . . . . N	0.387 . . . . . . R
1.15 L	38.7 I	7.3 . . . . F
0.4 . . . . K	0.115 C	0.52 . . . . N
0.999 . . . . . R	0.9 . . . . B	0.09 . . . . O

Riddle Answer

A ___ ___ ___ ___ ___ ___ ___ ___ ___ ___

4 **7** **10** **9** **2** **3** **6** **5** **8** **1**

NAME_____ DATE_____

Riddle 32

Why didn't anyone listen to the balloon that bragged?

What To Do

Fill in the blanks with the equivalent fraction, decimal, or percent. Match each answer to a letter in the Key. Then write the letter in the space above its problem number to find the answer to the riddle.

1 $\frac{1}{2}$ = 0.5 = _____

2 $\frac{4}{5}$ = _____ = 80%

3 _____ = 0.75 = 75%

4 $\frac{7}{8}$ = 0.875 = _____

5 _____ = 0.2 = 20%

6 $\frac{1}{10}$ = _____ = 10%

7 $\frac{69}{100}$ = 0.69 = _____

8 $\frac{100}{100}$ = _____ = 100%

9 _____ = 0.16 = 16%

10 $\frac{1}{3}$ = 0.333 = _____

Key

0.1 L	0.4 . . . . D	$^1/_5$ I
1 . . . . T	50% . . . . F	$^3/_4$ . . . . A
$^4/_{25}$ . . . . O	0.8 L	$^1/_2$ . . . . G
0.2 V	875% . . . . G	$^1/_{16}$ . . . . U
33.3% . . . . . . H	69% . . . . O	87.5% . . . . . R

Riddle Answer

It was fu __ __ __ __ __ __ __ __ __ __ __ __.

   2   **6**   **7**   **1**   **10**   **9**   **8**   **3**   **5**   **4**

NAME _____ DATE _____

Riddle 33

What did the mouse say to his kids to get them to pose for a picture?

What To Do

In each problem, circle the decimal or percent that is greater. Match each answer to a letter in the Key. Then write the letter in the space above its problem number to find the answer to the riddle.

1 0.10 or **100%**

2 0.4 or **30%**

3 0.8 or **75%**

4 0.62 or **5%**

5 0.27 or **32%**

6 0.02 or **20%**

7 0.19 or **17%**

8 0.06 or **5%**

9 0.44 or **39%**

10 0.78 or **82%**

Key

100%	A	82%	S	0.19	Y
0.44	S	0.8	Y	0.4	C
20%	H	0.10	O	0.06	E
75%	P	0.62	E	0.02	T
32%	E	30%	N	5%	W

Riddle Answer

"He ___ , ___ ___ ___ ___ ___ ___ ___ ___ ___!"
3　　**10** **1** **7**　　**2** **6** **8** **4** **9** **5**

NAME_____   DATE_____

Riddle 34

What did the wind say before blowing out the candle?

What To Do

In each problem, circle the percent or fraction that is greater.
Match each answer to a letter in the Key. Then write the letter in the space
above its problem number to find the answer to the riddle.

1 50% or $\frac{3}{4}$

2 20% or $\frac{3}{5}$

3 40% or $\frac{6}{20}$

4 60% or $\frac{4}{10}$

5 90% or $\frac{7}{7}$

6 15% or $\frac{11}{100}$

7 37% or $\frac{14}{50}$

8 64% or $\frac{4}{5}$

9 21% or $\frac{3}{25}$

10 48% or $\frac{11}{22}$

Key

37% . . . . T	50% . . . . W	$^3/_4$ I
21% . . . . S	$^6/_{20}$ . . . . D	$^7/_7$ L
64% . . . . A	40% . . . . T	15% . . . . U
$^{11}/_{22}$ . . . . S	$^4/_5$ . . . . H	60% . . . . G
$^3/_5$ . . . . O	48% . . . . P	$^4/_{10}$ . . . . K

Riddle Answer

"It' __ __ __ __ __ __ __ __ __ __ __ !"
    10 **5** **1** **4** **8** **7** **9** **2** **6** **3**

NAME _____   DATE _____

Riddle 35

Why did the cat sleep so well in his new bed?

What To Do

Answer the questions below. Match each answer to a letter in the Key. Then write the letter in the space above its problem number to find the answer to the riddle.

1 What percent of these shapes is a square? _____   □ △

2 What percent of these shapes are squares? _____   □△△○○○ ☆☆☆☆

3 What percent of these shapes are triangles? _____   △□□□□

4 What percent of these shapes are circles? _____   ☆○□△○ △○△☆□

5 What percent of these shapes are stars? _____   ☆△○○

6 What percent of these circles are shaded? _____   ○○●○○○○●○○ ○○○○●○○○○○

7 What percent of these squares are NOT shaded? _____   ▩□▩□▩□▩□▩ □▩□▩□▩□▩

8 What percent of these shapes are stars AND triangles? _____   □☆☆△△○△□□□○○ ○☆△○☆○□□○□□□

Key

45%	C
40%	B
50%	P
32%	U
5%	X
20%	R
3%	F
4%	C
25%	T
30%	R
10%	F
15%	E

Riddle Answer:

The bed was ___ ___ ___ ___ – ___ ___ ___ ___ !

① ⑧ ④ ③   ② ⑥ ⑦ ⑤

NAME_____ DATE _____

Riddle 36

Why was the backhoe so good at finding things?

What To Do

Solve the percent problems below. Match each answer to a letter in the Key. Then write the letter in the space above its problem number to find the answer to the riddle.

1 10% of 100 = _____

2 10% of 10 = _____

3 10% of 20 = _____

4 10% of 50 = _____

5 10% of 30 = _____

6 10% of 650 = _____

7 10% of 320 = _____

8 10% of 200 = _____

9 10% of 400 = _____

10 10% of 9,000 = _____

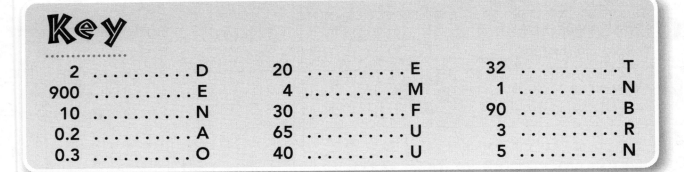

Key

2 . . . . D	20 . . . . E	32 . . . . T
900 . . . . E	4 . . . . M	1 . . . . N
10 . . . . N	30 . . . . F	90 . . . . B
0.2 . . . . A	65 . . . . U	3 . . . . R
0.3 . . . . O	40 . . . . U	5 . . . . N

Riddle Answer

It left no sto __ __   __ __ __ __ __ __ __ __ __ __ .
        1 8   6 4 7 9 5 2 10 3

NAME_____   DATE_____

Riddle 37

Why was the piece of clothing so hard to find?

What To Do

Solve the percent problems below. Match each answer to a letter in the Key. Then write the letter in the space above its problem number to find the answer to the riddle.

1 20% of $86 = _____

2 15% of $64 = _____

3 7% of $49 = _____

4 31% of $75 = _____

5 3% of $12 = _____

6 42% of $5 = _____

7 19% of $50 = _____

8 60% of $11 = _____

9 75% of $33 = _____

10 58% of $82 = _____

Key

$17.50 V	$0.36 . . . . S	$6.60 . . . . A
$3.43 . . . . . . R	$9.50 . . . . E	$2.10 . . . . N
$9.60 . . . . . . R	$17.20 . . . . D	$24.75 . . . . E
$3.60 . . . . . . P	$34.30 . . . . G	$3.25 L
$47.56 . . . . . . U	$23.75 . . . . O	$23.25 . . . . . W

Riddle Answer

It wa __ __ __ __ __ __ __ __ __ __ __ __ __ __.

5   **10** **6** **1** **9** **3**   **4** **7** **8** **2**

NAME_____ DATE_____

Riddle 38

What did the cat say when she stepped on a sharp rock?

What To Do

Solve the word problems below. Match each answer to a letter in the Key. Then write the letter in the space above its problem number to find the answer to the riddle.

1 Dana has two $1 bills and 50¢ in coins. How much money does she have? _____

2 Julio has one $5 bill, three $1 bills, and 20¢ in coins. How much money does he have? _____

3 Hannah has $4.50. Max has $6.10. How much money do they have together? _____

4 Sarita has $1.25. She finds 75¢ on the sidewalk. How much money does she have now? _____

5 Donovan has $9.40. Lilly has $6.00. How much more money does Donovan have than Lilly? _____

6 Olivia has $5.00. Emma has $4.30. How much more money does Olivia have than Emma? _____

7 Tony has $11.17. Chris has $20.34. John has $32.08. How much money do they all have together? _____

8 Leah has $7.35. Then she doubles the amount of money she has. How much money does she have now? _____

9 José has three times more money than Bob. Bob has $5.25 cents. How much money does José have? _____

10 Brian has half the amount of money Russell has. Russell has $28.22. How much money does Brian have? _____

Key

$1.50	I
$3.40	W
$10.60	A
$14.11	H
$15.25	F
$63.59	R
70¢ . . .	U
$10.50	G
$14.70	O
$3.50	D
$15.75	T
$6.20	E
$2.00	H
$8.20	T
$2.50	T

Riddle Answer "Me- __ __ ! __ __ __ __ __ __ __ __ __ __!"
8 5   2 4 3 9   10 6 7 1

NAME _____ DATE _____

Riddle 39

What did the left foot say to the right foot?

What To Do

Solve the word problems below. Match each answer to a letter in the Key. Then write the letter in the space above its problem number to find the answer to the riddle.

1 Steve weighs 175 pounds. Charlie weighs 150.3 pounds. How much more does Steve weigh than Charlie? _____

2 Carla is 5 feet, 6 inches tall. Taiyo is 4 feet, 8 inches tall. What is their combined height? _____

3 Wendell hits a baseball 44.8 feet. Larry hits a baseball half as far as Wendell does. How far does Larry hit a baseball? _____

4 Nick weighs 85.5 pounds. He gains 17.25 pounds over the next 2 years. How much does he weigh after 2 years? _____

5 Keisha is 6 feet tall. Jane is 6 feet, 2 inches tall. Francine is 4 feet, 11 inches tall. How much taller is Keisha than Francine? _____

6 Viktor's dog weighs 6 times more than Christina's cat. Viktor's dog weighs 33 pounds. How much does Christina's cat weigh? _____

7 Becky weighs 68.75 pounds. Kendra weighs twice as much as Becky. What is their combined weight? _____

8 Building A has 84 floors. Building B has 25 percent the number of floors Building A has. How many floors does Building B have? _____

9 A neighborhood has 100 homes. Four months later, it has 122 homes. By what percentage did the number of homes in the neighborhood grow? _____

10 Tomas weighs 108.5 pounds. Matt weighs 123 pounds. Carlos weighs 97.75 pounds. Oliver weighs 112.5 pounds. Who weighs less: Tomas and Oliver or Matt and Carlos? _____

Key

5.5 pounds	O
102.75 pounds	S
16%	M
22.4 feet	P
Matt and Carlos	S
10 feet, 2 inches	E
20 floors	A
24.7 pounds	I
Tomas and Oliver	L
206.25 pounds	T
21 floors	T
1 foot, 1 inch taller	N
2 feet, 1 inch taller	R
22 percent	T
137.5 pounds	Q

Riddle Answer "Le __ ' __ __ __ __ __ __ __ __ __ __!"

7 **4** **10 8 2 3** **6 5** **1 9**

NAME _____ DATE _____

Riddle 40

What did the shivering barn do to get warm?

What To Do

Solve the word problems below. Match each answer to a letter in the Key. Then write the letter in the space above its problem number to find the answer to the riddle.

1 Miguel finished a 100-meter race in 11.2 seconds. Peter finished in 11.8 seconds. How much faster was Miguel's time than Peter's? _____

2 Carol completed a test 12.4 seconds after Laura did. Laura completed the test in 25 minutes, 4.3 seconds. How long did it take Carol to complete the test? _____

3 Frank tied his shoes in 6.353 seconds. Sam tied his shoes in 6.062 seconds. Who took longer? _____

4 Mel ran around the block in 4 minutes, 22 seconds. Raquel took twice as long as Mel. How long did it take Raquel? _____

5 Ben watches TV for half the time Tam does. Tam watches for 2 hours, 36 minutes. How long does Ben watch for? _____

6 Ian, Jim, Wendy, and David ran a 400-meter relay race. Ian ran 100 meters in 13.2 seconds. Jim ran it in 11.9 seconds, Wendy in 12.5 seconds, and David in 12.7 seconds. What was their combined time? _____

7 Cliff hiked up a mountain in 6 hours. Leo took a short cut and finished in 25% less time than Cliff. How long did it take Leo to hike up the mountain? _____

8 Marta, Ichiro, Henry, and Dani ran a 400-meter relay race in 58.8 seconds. Each runner took the same amount of time to run 100 meters. How fast did each runner run? _____

Key

14.7 seconds	I
Sam	C
25 minutes, 16.7 seconds	T
50.3 seconds	N
Frank	A
4.5 hours	T
13 minutes, 9 seconds	S
6 seconds	D
8 minutes, 44 seconds	O
0.6 seconds	P
1.5 hours	U
1 hour, 18 minutes	A

Riddle Answer   Put on a c  __ __ __ of  __ __ __ __ __

④ ⑤ ②   ① ③ ⑧ ⑥ ⑦

Answers

Riddle 1 (page 5)
1. 5
2. 0
3. 6
4. 7
5. 2
6. 8
7. 4
8. 1
9. 3
10. 9

What do you call a tree root with four equal sides?
A square root

Riddle 2 (page 6)
1. 2
2. 5
3. 8
4. 4
5. 1
6. 10
7. 12
8. 9
9. 20
10. 14

Why did the farmer want the tree, instead of his dog, to guard his sheep?
The tree had more bark.

Riddle 3 (page 7)
1. 2.4
2. 6.8
3. 5.1
4. 10.8
5. 1.9
6. 17.2
7. 25.5
8. 8.3
9. 30.1
10. 12.7

What did the blanket say to the bed?
"I've got you covered."

Riddle 4 (page 8)
1. 5.26
2. 7.85
3. 10.63
4. 8.47
5. 3.99
6. 2.16
7. 15.78
8. 1.37
9. 20.55
10. 9.12

Why did the Earth make the sun dizzy?
It went around in circles.

Riddle 5 (page 9)
1. 6.2
2. 3.1
3. 4.48
4. 7.63
5. 9.08
6. 15.4
7. 5.658
8. 20.83
9. 32.461
10. 75.1

What did the bee say before eating its favorite meal?
"Thanks, honey!"

Riddle 6 (page 10)
1. 0.1
2. 0.5
3. 0.7
4. 0.18
5. 0.25
6. 0.01
7. 0.6
8. 0.99
9. 0.463
10. 0.003

How can the pots tell when the kettle is mad?
It blows off steam.

Riddle 7 (page 11)
1. 0.4
2. 0.25
3. 0.5
4. 0.125
5. 0.7
6. 0.2
7. 0.06
8. 0.525
9. 0.75
10. 0.03

What did the rabbit say to get the other rabbits moving?
"Let's hop to it!"

Riddle 8 (page 12)
1. 1/10
2. 3/10
3. 1/2
4. 4/5
5. 1/5
6. 3/5
7. 1/4
8. 37/100
9. 23/50
10. 3/25

What did the cow say to the tractor that was blocking its path?
"Please moo-ve."

Riddle 9 (page 13)
1. 5.1
2. 4.7
3. 26.5
4. 12.45
5. 35.16
6. 67.08
7. 95.48
8. 17.031
9. 59.675
10. 186.005

Why did the window succeed in business?
It was always open.

Riddle 10 (page 14)
1. 4.5
2. 1.75
3. 5.8
4. 2.3
5. 10.25
6. 8.875
7. 12.625
8. 3.75
9. 6.5
10. 20.4
What is a dog's favorite
type of clothing?
A pair of pants

Riddle 11 (page 15)
1. 0.58
2. 3/4
3. 6/10
4. 9/20
5. 0.93
6. 14/56
7. 7/8
8. 15/40
9. 1/10
10. 0.536
Why was the tired criminal
glad when the cops came?
He was now under ar-rest.

Riddle 12 (page 16)
1. 1.5
2. 4.6
3. 8.91
4. 5.83
5. 0.29
6. 0.47
7. 7.124
8. 9.658
9. 83.065
10. 10.003
Why did the phone stop calling
the answering machine?
It never returned messages.

Riddle 13 (page 17)
1. 4.4
2. 8.7
3. 13.5
4. 13.3
5. 11.1
6. 18.25
7. 16.67
8. 23.93
9. 28.542
10. 41.816
Why was the bird afraid to fly?
It was a scared-crow.

Riddle 14 (page 18)
1. 0.7
2. 1
3. 1.1
4. 0.8
5. 1.2
6. 18.8
7. 17.4
8. 13.4
9. 36.1
10. 42.3
Why did the salad feel naked?
It didn't have any dressing.

Riddle 15 (page 19)
1. 0.67
2. 0.7
3. 9.9
4. 12.87
5. 18.26
6. 0.677
7. 1.874
8. 17.404
9. 28.165
10. 31.998
Which planet won the
singing contest?
It was Nep-tune.

Riddle 16 (page 20)
1. 3.63
2. 0.706
3. 15.88
4. 0.599
5. 1.927
6. 32.812
7. 15.096
8. 109.874
9. 93.742
10. 53.348

Why was the hockey player
always in trouble?
He skated on thin ice.

Riddle 17 (page 21)
1. 14
2. 4
3. 7
4. 15
5. 18
6. 3
7. 9
8. 11
9. 44
10. 209
Why is it hard to listen
to a circle speak?
It never gets to the point.

Riddle 18 (page 22)
1. 0.1
2. 0.4
3. 0.2
4. 0.5
5. 0.7
6. 3
7. 4.7
8. 0.8
9. 1.8
10. 5.6
What did the shovel say
to the sick bucket?
"You look pail!"

Riddle 19 (page 23)
1. 1.5
2. 2.3
3. 1.7
4. 4.4
5. 7.6
6. 2.9
7. 4.3
8. 9.1
9. 0.8
10. 11.2
Why did the horse
keep stopping?
It was a stall-ion.

Riddle 20 (page 24)
1. 4.5
2. 3.8
3. 1.7
4. 3.6
5. 2.9
6. 12.2
7. 22.4
8. 47.3
9. 4.1
10. 46.7
Why was the shirt sad?
Because it was blue.

Riddle 21 (page 25)
1. 0.22
2. 0.1
3. 0.52
4. 0.032
5. 0.814
6. 3.24
7. 15.08
8. 2.39
9. 10.362
10. 0.345
What do boxers do
before going to bed?
They have a pillow fight.

Riddle 22 (page 26)
1. 6.44
2. 15.06
3. 4.31
4. 9.42
5. 5.454
6. 33.938
7. 8.776
8. 17.21
9. 11.269
10. 4.278
Why did the father keep
giving his children candy?
He was a lolli-pop.

Riddle 23 (page 27)
1. 0.2
2. 4
3. 4.2
4. 48
5. 72.1
6. 19
7. 37.8
8. 18.9

9. 51
10. 73.8
Why didn't anyone
trust the lamp?
It was shady.

Riddle 24 (page 28)
1. 32.15
2. 11.8
3. 30.48
4. 93.6
5. 97.6
6. 56.7
7. 114.88
8. 230.12
9. 210
10. 357
What fruit is round, red,
and always puts its best
foot forward?
A red toma-toe

Riddle 25 (page 29)
1. 0.25
2. 0.32
3. 0.14
4. 0.57
5. 1.98
6. 3.92
7. 5.25
8. 17.2558
9. 41.2296
10. 43.3026
What did the dog say to the other
dog before sharing his food?
"Bone appetit!"

Riddle 26 (page 30)
1. 0.365
2. 0.064
3. 0.1701
4. 0.8924
5. 11.0276
6. 1.2191
7. 5.205
8. 37.16295
9. 30.03616
10. 9.56672
Why did the truck quit working
at the construction site?
**It was tired of being
dumped on.**

Riddle 27 (page 31)
1. 10
2. 8
3. 15
4. 20
5. 25
6. 16
7. 50
8. 12
9. 65
10. 30
Why was the fish asked
to tell jokes?
It was a clown fish.

Riddle 28 (page 32)
1. 0.2
2. 2.5
3. 4.75
4. 4
5. 6.125
6. 67
7. 5
8. 9.5
9. 3.4
10. 6.5
What did the elephant
say about the flies?
"They really bug me!"

Riddle 29 (page 33)
1. 3.875
2. 4
3. 6.25
4. 12.16
5. 9.34
6. 10.07
7. 7.338
8. 204.5
9. 57.89
10. 321.2
Why do frogs celebrate
every four years?
It's leap year!

Riddle 30 (page 34)
1. 30%
2. 15%
3. 7%
4. 29%
5. 41%
6. 6%
7. 97%
8. 37.5%

9. 86.1%
10. 1.2%
Why did the tree that was
in business grow more limbs?
It wanted to branch out.

Riddle 31 (page 35)
1. 0.52
2. 0.88
3. 0.73
4. 0.04
5. 0.09
6. 0.115
7. 0.262
8. 0.387
9. 0.999
10. 0.4319
Which vegetable listens well?
An ear of corn

Riddle 32 (page 36)
1. 50%
2. 0.8
3. 3/4
4. 87.5%
5. 1/5
6. 0.1
7. 69%
8. 1
9. 4/25
10. 33.3%
Why didn't anyone listen to the
balloon that bragged?
It was full of hot air.

Riddle 33 (page 37)
1. 100%
2. 0.4
3. 0.8
4. 0.62
5. 32%
6. 20%
7. 0.19
8. 0.06
9. 0.44
10. 82%
What did the mouse say to
his kids to get them to pose
for a picture?
"Hey, say cheese!"

Riddle 34 (page 38)
1. 3/4
2. 3/5
3. 40%
4. 60%
5. 7/7
6. 15%
7. 37%
8. 4/5
9. 21%
10. 11/22
What did the wind say before
blowing out the candle?
"It's lights out!"

Riddle 35 (page 39)
1. 50%
2. 10%
3. 20%
4. 30%
5. 25%
6. 15%
7. 45%
8. 32%
Why did the cat sleep
so well in his new bed?
The bed was purr-fect!

Riddle 36 (page 40)
1. 10
2. 1
3. 2
4. 5
5. 3
6. 65
7. 32
8. 20
9. 40
10. 900
Why was the backhoe so
good at finding things?
It left no stone unturned.

Riddle 37 (page 41)
1. $17.20
2. $9.60
3. $3.43
4. $23.25
5. $0.36
6. $2.10
7. $9.50
8. $6.60
9. $24.75
10. $47.56

Why was the piece of
clothing so hard to find?
It was under wear.

Riddle 38 (page 42)
1. $2.50
2. $8.20
3. $10.60
4. $2.00
5. $3.40
6. 70¢
7. $63.59
8. $14.70
9. $15.75
10. $14.11
What did the cat say when she
stepped on a sharp rock?
"Me-ow! That hurt!"

Riddle 39 (page 43)
1. 24.7 pounds
2. 10 feet, 2 inches
3. 22.4 feet
4. 102.75 pounds
5. 1 foot, 1 inch taller
6. 5.5 pounds
7. 206.25 pounds
8. 21 floors
9. 22 percent
10. Matt and Carlos
What did the left foot say
to the right foot?
"Let's step on it!"

Riddle 40 (page 44)
1. 0.6 seconds
2. 25 minutes, 16.7 seconds
3. Frank
4. 8 minutes, 44 seconds
5. 1 hour, 18 minutes
6. 50.3 seconds
7. 4.5 hours
8. 14.7 seconds
What did the shivering barn
do to get warm?
Put on a coat of paint